When I was a child, I spoke as a child, I understood as a child, and I thought as a child, but when I became a Man, I put away childish things.

I Corinthians 13:11

*

*

That we henceforth be no more children

Ephesians 4:14

Sensitive Saints

Overcoming the Spirit of Offense

Vol.1

Bishop Jeffrey L. Melvin

Foreword by Bishop James R. Wright, Sr., PhD

Prepared by Ebony Nicole Smith Consulting, LLC | ebonynicolesmith.com

Editor: AB Brumfield

Cover Design: Faith Works | Lois T. M. Gaines

All Scripture was used from the King James Version of the Bible | ©2012 by Barbour Publishing, Inc.

ISBN: 9798326942074

Printed in the United States of America

First printing, 2024

Contents

Sensitive Saints

Dedication

I am dedicating this book to my wife, Deborah, daughter Brittany, and five Godchildren: Jamal Briggs-Donaldson, Paul Marshall Hogan III, Selah Yvette Long, and Soleh Kaylee Long. This book is also dedicated to my Godson, Jaleon Jeffrey Tate, who is now residing inside Heaven's gates.

And to our nearly two hundred nieces, nephews, great-nieces, and nephews, this book is dedicated to you, too.

Deborah and I love you all with all of our hearts.

Foreword

• • •

During the forty years that I have known Bishop Jeffrey Melvin, I have experienced him as a dedicated, studious, inquisitive, and loyal servant of God. As such, I felt led by God to appoint him as my special assistant in the New York Western First Ecclesiastical Jurisdiction of the Church of God in Christ.

I am very excited about his new book, *Sensitive Saints: Overcoming the Spirit Offense*. In these unique times that we live in, this book is needed to assist believer in their Christian walk. It is a concise, direct, and to-the-point examination of the spirit of offense and how the people of God can be conquerors. Not only has he identified many areas of offense in the life of a believer, but he also offered powerful remedies and helpful tools to be victorious over this debilitating spirit.

As you read this book, I pray that you receive his insight. I also pray that you will be delivered from any of Satan's attempts to cause offense to linger and hinder God's growth in your life. Please share this book with others so that they may be delivered and set free just as you were from the powerful writing of Bishop Jeffrey Melvin.

“But I have prayed for thee, that thy faith fail not: and when thou art converted, strengthen thy brethren.”
Luke 22:32 (KJV)

Bishop James R. Wright, Sr., PhD, Presiding Prelate New York Western First Ecclesiastical Jurisdiction Church of God in Christ

Introduction

In the Beginning, There Was an Offense

•••

Genesis is the book of the Genes, where all things under the sun begin. In that book, we find two brothers, Cain, the eldest, and Abel, the younger. Both Cain and Abel were the sons of Adam, the son of creation, and Eve, the mother of all mankind.

Because of sin, labor was thrust upon mankind within the confines of hard physical labor for men and the tribulation of child birthing for women. It was also the promise of living as a reward. If you labor as God commanded, there will be fruit, vegetation, and livestock. You shall receive a day's pay if you work a day's work. All of your labor shall be compensated for your effort. It's all yours, except for that portion that you must repay to God (Malachi 3:8-12). Repaying or returning the tithes to God frees God's hand to restock or re-seed you so that you may continue the cycle. In addition, tithing also shows gratitude toward Him.

When we obey God, we become blessed, happy, prospered, content, joyful, joyous, satisfied, assured, anticipatory, and generous, along with many of His blessings.

When we disobey God in any area, we become anxious, cold, suspicious, cranky,
nervous, withdrawn, secluded, excluded, jealous, vengeful, bitter, and yes, sensitive.

You Are Hurting, Now What?

So, you're hurt.

Now what?

Do you quit, get upset, or get even? Do you get mad, become quiet, throw rocks, stay frustrated, or raise sand? Or do you find a way to process the hurt without falling into the bottomless pit of the *sensitive saint?*

The Spirit of Offense

Offense means to be offended, resentful or annoyed, typically due to a perceived insult. Not sensitive sinners or sensitive saints.

From Whence Cometh Wars? James 4:1-10:

"From whence come wars and fightings among you? come they not hence, even of your lusts that war in your members?

Ye lust, and have not: ye kill, and desire to have, and cannot obtain: ye fight and war, yet ye have not, because ye ask not.

Ye ask, and receive not, because ye ask amiss, that ye may consume it upon your lusts.

Ye adulterers and adulteresses, know ye not that the friendship of the world is enmity with God? whosoever therefore will be a friend of the world is the enemy of God.

Do ye think that the scripture saith in vain, The spirit that dwelleth in us lusteth to envy?
But he giveth more grace. Wherefore he saith, God resisteth the proud, but giveth grace unto the humble.
Submit yourselves therefore to God. Resist the devil, and he will flee from you.
Draw nigh to God, and he will draw nigh to you. Cleanse your hands, ye sinners; and purify your hearts, ye double-minded.
Be afflicted, and mourn, and weep: let your laughter be turned to mourning, and your joy to heaviness.
Humble yourselves in the sight of the Lord, and he shall lift you up."

From infancy we learn to become and sometimes to remain offended. We learn that it feels terrible to be laughed at, talked about, or even to be thought ill of. Having any of those things done to you feels like a size fifteen shoe kicking you in the gut! It's also unusually difficult to try to master those natural emotions. When we dig deep into the roots of our emotional stability (or lack thereof), we can almost always trace our challenges back to our childhood.

Now, let me pause for the cause and say that I'm not a clinician, psychologist, medical doctor, or practitioner. I'm a Pastor, a student of Scripture and of this thing we call life.

John 10:10 tells us that *"He has come that we might have life and have life more abundantly."* My desire is that you and I will live a well-balanced, Christ-centered life.

The word *life* in Greek is *zoe*, it means whole, spirited, blessed, complete life. We cannot live this type of life if we are constantly stuck on hurt or living the life of the offended. Too consistently our struggle with being offended leads to an over-sensitivity in our spirit. This causes us to become suspicious of everything and everybody. As a result, we withdraw from life because we are hurting. We will either have to let go or continue in the hurt. Believe me, I get it.

Hey, Fat Boy!

I had always been a big kid; in fact, I've been heavy all my life. It wasn't unusual for me to be the largest kid in all my classes. I wasn't big like a big, bad, bully big, but more like Fat Albert big or Baby Huey big. This type of big came with its own set of problems. I was always picked on and called terrible names by other kids; Fat Boy seemed to be a favorite used by my tormentors.

"Hey, Fat Boy!" "Give me your money, Fat Boy!" or, "I'm going to beat you up after school, Fat Boy!"

Yeah, the name Fat Boy stuck with me throughout the early segment of my life and set me up to be sensitive in a lot of areas. Even though my mother taught me valuable sayings like, "Sticks and stones may break my bones, but words will never hurt me," those words did hurt me, and they hurt deeply.

How we deal with those early defining times of embarrassment and rejection is paramount to how we deal with life's sensitive seasons. We have sensitive moments, sensitive periods, sensitive time frames, and sensitive seasons that can develop into a sensitive soul. Dealing with sensitive moments isn't something I just know how to do, that knowledge comes from lived experiences that I'll share more of later in the book.

Thinking about it, I remember that old Billie Holiday blues tune where she says, "Good morning, heartache, sit down." We must be sure we don't become conditioned by our circumstances to be comfortable with hurt, misery, and pain. Usually, we become so because we're not being watchful unto prayer (I Peter 4:7).

In my estimation, today is the most sensitive day in recorded history. One out of every four people is medicated for some type of anxiety. Manners and kindness have been tremendously depleted. Most people are led by their fears rather than by their faith, and we have lost our mettle. Our vigor, vim, and vitality have gotten up and been escorted to the door by our touchy feelings.

To Be Sensitive

Sensitive is defined as quick to detect or to respond to slight changes, signals, or influences.

In other words, to be sensitive means to respond very quickly to all kinds of stimuli or to the blowing of any kind of wind in your vicinity. To be overly sensitive is also a sign of immaturity. The Bible clearly commands us to be steadfast and unmovable and ever abounding in the faith (1 Corinthians 15:58).

Faith is the opposite of fear, sensitivity, and offense. The Bible also instructs that we no longer be children tossed to and fro by every wind of doctrine (Ephesians 4:14).

With insight, revelation, understanding, and lived experiences, in this volume of *Sensitive Saints: Overcoming the Spirit of Offense,* I want to scratch at least the surface of dealing with this vital challenge of our time.

Chapter 1

Cain, the Ultimate Sensitive Brother

• • •

With everything in life, we can trace its origin to the Book of the Genes. In Genesis 4, we find two brothers, Cane and Abel. One was a doer, while the other was a watcher. One was a producer, the other was a complainer, one a praiser, and the other a supplanter. One has life, and the other took life. One praised God, the other blamed God foolishly. One was satisfied; the other was hurt and sensitive. And why? Cain saw the favor of God in his brother's life and became sensitive and jealous about it. He felt that God loved Abel more than He loved him. His jealousy and sensitivity stemmed from how God received Abel's meat offering but rejected his grain offering.

Now, before you get deep on me and suppose that God rejected Cain's offering because it was not a more valuable offering of meat, as some theologians have argued, let me help you. God only requires us to give of what He's given to us. Abel sacrificed meat because it was his job to oversee the sheep. It was Cain's job to oversee the vegetation (Genesis 4). God never expects us to give an account for someone else's sacrifice, but instead we should give the best of our own sacrifice.

Cain became offended by his brother's success. He watched him prosper and grew more and more angry because of the blessings of God that fell on Abel and not on him.

While Cain brought what seemed to be the worst of his sacrifices, Abel gave to his God the best of his tithe and offerings. The younger brother showed God that he valued all that God had done for him by allowing him to labor for Him. God did not respect Cain's giving because he gave it in the wrong spirit, a spirit of competition and offense, thereby incurring anger and rejection of God.

In Gen 4:6, God asked Cain, *"Why are you angry (offended)? Why is your expression downcast?"* Or, like my Momma used to say, "Why is your face all twisted up?" Of course, God knew exactly what was wrong with Cain, just like He knows precisely what is wrong with us when we are offended. God then confronted Cain and tried to offer him a better way than the path of offense he had chosen. So God offered Cain a solution to his self-imposed offense. It's simple, *"If thou doeth well, shalt thou not be accepted? And if thou doeth not well, sin lies at the door. And unto thee shall be his desire, and thou shalt rule over him"* (Genesis 4:7). In other words, if you do what Abel is doing and stop being jealous and offended you will take your rightful place as firstborn.

Just think how many of us have lost our place because of the spirit of offense. So many times, our ire needs to be directed and addressed! When we don't address the person, we come in a spirit of anger because we make our own conditions and conclusions before hearing out the other person's matter. God literally gave Cain Godly council. God addressed the issue of his sensitivity and told him why Abel's sacrifice was acceptable and his was not.

This came down to a matter of Cain being satisfied with offering God his worst rather than his best. Instead of taking God's excellent council, Cain decided that he would murder his brother. That wasn't the end of his troubles though, because the God who knows all and sees all confronted Cain again, this time inquiring about the whereabouts of his brother.

Genesis 4:9-11 KJV

"And the Lord said unto Cain, "Where is Abel thy brother?"
His reply was swift and ill-stated at the same time.
"I know not: am I my brother's keeper?"
And he said, "What hast thou done? The voice of thy brother's blood crieth unto me from the ground. And now thou art cursed from the earth, which hath opened her mouth to receive thy brother's blood from thy hand."

Cain's spirit of jealousy turned into offense, which turned into malice, which resulted in murder!

Chapter 2

Envy, the Breeding Ground for Hate

•••

Psalms 73:3 says, "I was envious of *the foolish when I saw the prosperity of the foolish."*

Envy is feeling discontented or resentful, aroused by someone else's possessions, qualities, or good fortune.

To me, envy is one of the most dangerous, hideous, self-hating spirits a person can possess. It is even more egregious when the person exhibiting the spirit is a born-again believer. There's a lot to unpack in the short yet powerful scripture of Psalm 73:3, but let's attempt to break down the challenge our psalmist was facing.

He stated that he was envious of the foolish. This speaks to the fact that he realized his envy was not based on anything that was worth the squandering of his time, peace, sanity, and salvation.

God blesses the person who not only has come to the light of that fact but also realizes that what they were watching and feeling was not worthy of them becoming overly hurt or super sensitive. This brings me to the second point about why the psalmist became envious of what he saw. He looked over the fence at what his neighbor had and became very envious because he didn't have the same.

The Bible tells us that we should walk by faith and not by sight (2 Corinthians 5:7). One of the main ways to fall into the spirit of envy is by glaring at, longing for, and being jealous of what God has blessed others to accomplish, possess, or be privy to. Notice the B clause of that verse is *while watching.* It is virtually impossible to walk by faith and simultaneously catch feelings because of what others have.

I have a close relative who shall go unnamed. They constantly bump into people, tables, light poles, and many other things. The reason? They habitually walk forward while looking backward to see what they may have missed when they passed that location the first time.

I often tell them, "Hey, you can't walk forward while looking backward."

Likewise, just as you can't physically walk forward while looking backward, you can't do it emotionally either. You can't walk by faith and be envious or jealous of others. If you do, you'll begin to point the finger at others because you don't have what they have or because you haven't done what they've done. If you keep walking forward while looking back, you'll start asking God stupid questions. Yes, there really are stupid questions. Questions like, "Why them and not me?" and "Why were they hired and not me?" "How come their children are doing so well in school and mine aren't?" "Why did God favor them and not me?"

Once your frustration mounts and your envy goes unresolved, the seed of discontentment will grow into bitterness. When left undelivered, your bitterness will turn into hate—pure, sinful hate—and for what? Because you had your eyes and heart pointed in the wrong direction and as a result you locked into the wrong thing.

Envy is indeed the breeding ground of hate!

Chapter 3

Ahab, the Sensitive King

• • •

How sensitive do you think someone in power can become? Surprisingly, they can become sensitive to the point of murder. 1 Kings 21 reveals to us a King named Ahab and his Queen, Jezebel. From his depiction in the Bible, King Ahab was a weak-willed, insecure, jelly-backed, overly sensitive weakling of a man, a husband, a king, and a human. Being a perfect match to her husband, Queen Jezebel was a manipulative, mean-spirited, jealous-hearted, wicked, scheming, sensitive, devil-worshiping brute of a human. It's clear they were a couple that was equally yoked.

Like many powerful men in his time, King Ahab had the world at his fingertips, unlimited silver and gold, the finest garments, the best transportation of his day, the best cooks, multiple wives, and the best house in the neighborhood. During that day, a lot of value was placed on agriculture, particularly livestock, vegetation, and vineyards. Those vineyards were valued because the finest wines and beverages could be and often was made from them.

It just so happened that the king had a private vineyard. One of his citizens, a man named Naboth, whose name meant prominent, distinctive, flourishing, fruitful, and increase, also grew a vineyard right next to the king's. The Lord was certainly with Naboth as the man actually lived up to his name in every respect. We don't find Naboth glaring jealously at what the king had. On the contrary, we see ole jealous-hearted, weak-willed Ahab boohooing over the God-blessed vineyard of Naboth. In fact, the king was so envious and jealous of his neighbor's vineyard that he offered to trade with him and give him what he called a "better vineyard." However, Naboth possessed some things Ahab obviously did not have.

Loyalty, faithfulness, appreciation, and integrity defined his character. Because of that, Naboth unashamedly told Ahab in no uncertain terms that *"the Lord forbid it of me, that I should give the inheritance of my fathers unto thee"* (1 Kings 21:3). This refusal by Naboth to foolishly squander that which the Lord had blessed his family to possess for what appears to be generations, caused the sensitive jelly-backed king to go into a deep, dark hissy fit of depression.

Ahab's depression was on such a low level that he retreated to his king's chambers, fell across his bed, and sulked like a spoiled baby. His moaning and sulking were so wretched and pitiful that his wife Jezebel had to probe to find out just what was ailing her weak-backed husband.

Jezebel inquired as to the reason for this deep, dark depression. "What could be the cause of you confining yourself to the bed, and what's up with this hunger strike?"

His broken heartedness was so bad that he refused to even eat anything. With a broken heart and confused mind, he whiningly said, *"Because I spoke to Naboth the Jezereelite and said unto to him give me thy vineyard for money or else, if it please thee, I will give thee another vineyard for it: he answered I will not give thee my vineyard."* So the queen told Ahab, *"Rise and eat, you are the King, don't worry I'll get that vineyard for you from Naboth."*

Ahab's sensitivity, jealousy, and envy caused him and his wife to conspire against Naboth. They lied, connived, and connected with other evil people to rob that innocent man of his property, his inheritance, and his life.

As I write this book, I wonder if you know of others who have altered the lives of innocent folks because of misguided sensitivities and emotions. More pointedly, I wonder if you have been guilty of thinking that someone did not deserve that promotion, a new person in their life, or that position in the church, and because of misguided sensitivities, you killed them? Oh yes, I'm talking to you!

You may say, "Bishop Melvin, I've never killed anyone in my whole life."

Okay, you may not have physically killed them by a gun, knife, or hand grenade, but did you kill off their influence, their favor? Did you kill off their popularity by saying how they didn't deserve what they got and that you should have been the one shown that grace?

We often don't realize that if God can bless one, He can certainly bless all. Many times, it's just not our time to receive that particular grace. God knows what time is the best time for each of us to be blessed, so let's stop looking at others with suspicious eyes and start celebrating the fact that our God is able to cause all grace to abound toward us and our families in due season.

Remember when I mentioned that I speak not from what I just so happened to know but instead from lived experiences? Well, I remember when I was being considered to become the jurisdictional Bishop in Rwanda, East Africa. Due to the actions of someone else, all international appointments were halted. This delayed my elevation for nearly a year. Needless to say, I was heartbroken because I had done all I was supposed to do to meet the elevation. Despite the hardship of that season in my life, I'm so thankful for the encouragement I received from many people, notably Bishop Leroy Anderson. He really encouraged me.

Bishop Anderson said, "Elder Melvin, don't let this shake your faith. This happened and had nothing to do with any wrongdoing on your behalf. It's going to happen; you just keep serving the Lord."

I made up my mind that I wasn't going to let the devil play with my mind over this thing. I refused to get sensitive and hate others who received their promotion on that go-round. In fact, I gladly helped my brothers celebrate their lofty promotions as though it was mine. Just as Bishop Anderson said, my time and promotion came soon after that. I've learned never, ever to be envious or jealous over anything that others have, own, or possess.

Yes, they killed Naboth, but God avenged his death, vindicated his conviction, and cleared his good name.

Beware because envy leads to hate, and hate leads to murder!

Chapter 4

Sensitive Saul, Insane with Jealousy

•••

Same Story. Different Characters.

And David went out whithersoever Saul sent him, and behaved himself wisely: and Saul set him up over the men of war and he was accepted by all of the people and also in the sight of Saul's servants; and it came to pass as they came, when, David was returned from the slaughter of the Philistines, that the women came out of all cities of Israel, singing and dancing, to meet king Saul, with tabrets, with joy and with instruments of music. And the women answered one another as they played and said, Saul has slain his thousands and David his ten thousand. And Saul was very wroth *(angry, mad, perplexed, hot, jealous, confused, murderous, and sensitive).*

Samuel 18:5-8

Once again, we find biblical examples of how not to feel, act, or respond to others' successes.

Like other surrounding countries who sought to have a leader, Saul became king after the peoples' will to have a ruler caused them to beg God for what He didn't will them to have. God warned the children of Israel that this king would draft their sons into his military and remand their daughters into his harem. They were also warned that he would load them with taxes. God told the people of Israel that Saul would be a king after their flesh but not after His heart. The people responded, *"Nay, but we will have a king"* (1 Sam 8:19).

As I explored the huge challenges faced by Saul, I found there were many. Outwardly, he fits the bill as one who looked and talked like a legitimate king. The Bible tells us that he was the tallest man in the land. In fact, he stood head and shoulders above every other man in all of Israel (1 Sam 10:23). Outwardly, he was statuesque and muscular. I can imagine him possessing a deep Barry White baritone voice that, when he talked, commanded everyone in the room's attention.

Although Saul appeared to be the man for the task, God's perfect will did not include him as the ruler over Israel. However, it is what the people desired. Saul was the picture of what a king should be—to an extent. The Bible reads that his heart was filled with rage, insecurities, uncertainties, and deep-seated sensitivities. Even with these truths, God loved Saul and allowed His anointing to rest upon him.

We find several instances in the Bible where God favored King Saul.

- His private anointing 1 Sam 10:1-8
- His public acceptance 10: 17-27
- His military victories 1 Sam: 11

King Saul may not have been God's first choice to become the country's ruler, but there was yet room for him to walk after the blessings of the Lord.

I read a book called "Leading From the Second Chair" by Mike Bonem and Roger Patterson years ago. In the book is a chapter titled *Leaving the Second Chair*. This particular book speaks directly to what Saul faced while being God's second choice, even though he had been seated first. What a tremendous challenge our flesh can have when playing the second chair position.

The second chair is really a musical term that refers to a person who is not lead on a particular song or musical set. The lead chair is considered to be the best on a particular instrument and thus is called the first chair. For example, the lead violinist sets the tone for the entire orchestra to follow, be it in tone, tempo, volume, or pitch. If all goes well, the first chair and the conductor will receive most of the pats on the back or applause for a job well done. In the awesome book I mentioned, the authors point out how important it is for the second chair to maintain its place in the orchestra's structure. The second chair fills in the gap and maintains the flow of the musical piece. The second chair is often as good as the first chair, but they are content to play their role as if second best for the betterment of the team.

How awesome would it be if the Saints would just lay aside their petty insecurities and walk in their calling for the kingdom's sake? Just think about how people wouldn't rush to knock the leader off of his or her leadership position because of their thirst for power. These feelings often arise due to believing one can do a better job or that the leader's time is up.

One of the most morbid things I can think of is a person who should be aiding, assisting, complementing, and supporting a leader or the person God has ordained to be the leader but are instead just waiting for that person's demise or downfall, so that they can step in and be applauded and celebrated in their stead. That was the case with Saul and David. When I see that behavior being displayed today, it makes me wonder how those people were raised.

I have absolutely no room in my heart or my head to be sensitive or jealous of my leaders. I've been blessed to be under outstanding leadership throughout my lifetime. Yes, I am a consecrated Bishop in the grand ole Church of God in Christ. I am also a Bishop who is content to be under leadership. Along with the churches that I pastor, Encouragement Centre in Buffalo, NY, and Power House Kingdom Cathedral Church of God in Christ located in Rochester, NY, I, and those ministries, am under the great leadership of the honorable Bishop James R Wright. Bishop Wright is the prelate of the New York Western First Ecclesiastical Jurisdiction.

After being elevated to the office of Bishop, I became free to simply move our churches out from NY Western and become our own stand-apart jurisdiction. Yet, I remained under Bishop Wright's leadership. I felt there was so much more I could learn and offer to the NY Western Jurisdiction. I really do believe that in the multitude of counsel, there is safety (Proverbs 11:14).

I will never forget April of 1986. During our annual spring conference, Bishop Frederick Douglass Washington, prelate of the Eastern New York Jurisdiction Church of God in Christ, was invited to be the keynote speaker for the conference. I think it is essential to note that Bishop Washington's nickname among the preachers was the "Prince of Preachers". When I tell you that he could flat-out preach, he really could preach! In fact, the only occupation that he ever had was that of a preacher.

He was the second presiding Bishop serving under presiding Bishop J.O. Patterson, Sr. The thing that impressed me most about Bishop Washington wasn't actually his preaching, it was his servitude to the second chair leader of the national church. During that service, as he preached, he said, "So many people are sitting around waiting on the leader to die when there is so much that you can accomplish. He, the leader, yet lives."

The elections in the Church of God in Christ run concurrently with the national elections. In each quadrennial, most church offices are up for election, including the office of the Presiding Bishop. In 1987, there was a big uproar about other Bishops who could be seeking that seat. On Friday night of the Holy Convocation, Bishop F. D. Washington stirred the crowd when he chose his topic: "*Who's Side Are You Leaning On? I'm Leaning On The Lord's Side."* The message was so spirited and inspiring that the Rev. Timothy Wright wrote his winning song, *Leaning on the Lord's Side*, because of it.

Bishop Washington never publicly challenged his leader, nor did he heed the foolish suggestions that he should try to unseat him during election time. He refused to become sensitive because of the roar of the crowd. So many people are just sitting around, feeling sensitive because the crowd's roar is not wailing out their names. These people are looking for other people's approval rather than our All-Mighty God's approval. The Apostle Jesus said they shall have their just reward for the attention they seek from man instead of God (Matthew 6:2). In other words, the vain approval they seek is the only reward they shall receive.

Don't seek the approval of man. (Acts 5:29)

Circling back to Saul, at the end of his maniacal tirade, he ended up seeking out the council of the witch of Endor (1 Samuel 28) because he refused to take the council of godly leadership. He found no peace or solace at his sad, sensitive end. He took his life falling by on his sword, committing suicide, and dying in disgrace and full of offensive feelings.

Chapter 5

Sarah, the Mother of the Faithless

• • •

The book of the Genes reveals a husband and wife named Abraham and Sarah. As we know, Abraham is known as the Father of the Faith. They were an upwardly mobile power couple. Abraham was a successful herdsman who had livestock, gold, and silver (Gen 13:2). With all the riches he had, Abraham lacked the one thing that counted as successful for any couple. Children. This was challenging for both Abraham and Sarah, but for different reasons. It was challenging for Sarah because it was considered shameful for a woman not to bring a child to term, specifically a male child, which would carry the man's legacy as an heir. The challenge for Abraham was that God had made a promise to him about his seed.

Between Genesis 15 and 21, we find a series of promises and challenges between God and Abraham. Gen 15:2 says, *"And Abraham said, "Behold, what wilt thou give me, seeing I go childless, and the one born in my house is mine heir." God answered Abraham and said unto him, "This shall not be thine heir but he that shall come forth out of thine own bowels shall be thine heir."* God said it, meant it, and was going to perform it.

For context and understanding, we can assume that Sarah knew what God said to her husband. It is understood that communication happens in a marriage. The real challenge here is that Sarah, in a highly faithless move, offered to help God by performing the word God gave to Abraham, which was that he would father his heir. Sarah offered her handmaid, a young Egyptian girl named Hagar, to her husband to create the child God promised Abraham she, Sarah, would give to him (Gen 16:1-2). I need to note that it was somewhat of a common practice during that period for husbands to have more than one partner or wife and for wives to have handmaids. I also need to note that the Mosaic Law had not yet been brought down from Mt. Sinai this time.

Abraham was a Chaldean and along with his wife Sarah, was raised by Babylonian customs and standards. What is understood is that when you move from your homeland to the promised land for your future children, what God says becomes first and foremost.

There is a great faith lesson here. In an effort to build and test our faith in Him and Him alone, many times God will nudge us out of our comfort zones and out of our spaces of familiarity. The biblical truth that we find at work with this promise is that the promise was without conditions. He simply promised to bless Abraham's seed (Genesis 12:1-3).

Sarah's faithlessness and insecurity were astounding. She thought it was alright to assist God in bringing His promise to Abraham to pass. This faithless plan was certain to backfire on Sarah just as any insecure and faithless act of the flesh. Sarah's selfish act caused the handmaid's son to be born first to Abraham. The boy, Ishmael, was born to the handmaiden Hagar. Ishmael, the son of the flesh, was born a full thirteen years before Isaac, the son of faith.

Sarah became very sensitive after her grand idea blew up in her face (Gen 16:5-6). She was the one who sent her husband into her handmaiden's tent to have sex in order to conceive a son. Notice that Sarah assumed she would just take the son and raise him as her own. Genesis 16 shows us that not only did she force Hagar on her husband, but she also blamed God for not following through on His promise. Genesis 16:2 reads, "*Sarah said unto Abram, behold now, the Lord hath restrained me from bearing: I pray thee go into my maid that I may obtain children by her.*"

How many times in life do we completely mess things up because of our lack of faith and patience when it comes to the word of God and the promises of God? Because God didn't move in Sarah's timing, she thought it was not robbery to play God for herself. After her dastardly lack of faith and epic fail were consummated, she despised, hated, loathed, and was incredibly jealous of her handmaiden. The spirit of offense was in full effect within her.

This situation begs the question: Should we be upset with the Lord when the source of our insecurities comes from our own wrongdoing or miscalculations? Things only got worse after Abraham went into Hagar's tent. By the way, we see no resistance from ole Abe about completely complying with Sarah's desire to commit this faithless act. (I'm just saying).

We find Momma Sarah all in her feelings after seeing Hagar's baby bump. Once again, she flipped the script of blame, this time to Abraham, saying to him in so many words, "I was so wrong, now let my wrong be on you, hubby, for what you have done!" So, of course, Abe caved into faithless Sarah and told her (because of her hypersensitivity) to, "...do to her as you please." (Gen 16:6 ESV).

Allow me to take a minute to draw a very important parallel between four biblical men/husbands who all exhibited a fatal character flaw during certain times in their life:

1. Adam
2. Abraham
3. Ahab
4. King Herod

Any biblical search will shine the light on the fact that each of these men, at one time in their lives, caved into the insecurities, sensitivities, and offended nature of their wives.

In the case of Abraham dealing with Sarah's handmaiden, I find it appalling that, as a father, Abraham stood spineless and refused to be the leader in his home. We see little to no attempt made on his part to protect his son from the confusion in his house. I find it equally terrible that Sarah, in her completely innate insecure jealousies and self-imposed hatred against her handmaid, allowed herself to put the very lives of two human beings in danger of having to survive alone in the vast wilderness. How dare you, as a wife, mother, or fellow woman, drive a wedge between a father and his child? Regardless of how or when they were conceived, once science proves that he (your husband, brother, boyfriend, cousin, or ex) is the father, no one should attempt to prevent that child or dad from being an integral part of that child's life and upbringing.

After the angel of the Lord told Abraham to allow Ishmael and his mother to be banished to the wilderness because of Sarah's sensitiveness and offense, God made of him a great nation due to the unconditional covenant that he made to Abraham. We now know that nation as the Arab nation. God's perfect will was executed even through the process of His permissive will.

Chapter 6

Identifying the Root of Your Issues

• • •

Earlier in this book, I told you there were issues I would revisit. So, here we go!

I had to deal with my sensitivities, the parts of my life that caused me to walk in the spirit of offense. As I peeled away the layers, I uncovered the realization that when I was six years old and my parents split up, their separation made me feel vulnerable, hurt, unwanted, and sensitive.

When a child has a parent that leaves their life for whatever reason, some way, somehow, that child takes on a level of guilt and, yes, even shame. It has been reported that a child's personality develops by age five. Ingrained in that personality is also the emotional and psychological damage that whatever trauma may have occurred by that point has caused. In my case, I've always been an overweight child, so I quickly started hearing the sneer "Fat Boy". As a result, I became very sensitive about being overweight. Whenever I would hear the term fat boy being hollered out, I always knew the perpetrator was talking about me!

I was the neighborhood *fat boy*. My weight was a very sensitive issue for me. It attacked my self-confidence and my self-worth. It attacked my ability to deal with peers and disabled my ability to interact with adults. Let's not even mention the brutal cold shoulder treatment that one gets from the girls in school when you are an overweight kid.

I recall the one thing that gave my self-esteem a boost: performances. I would be given speeches and parts in plays during the Resurrection and Christmas programs. The saints' applause at the Prayer House Church of God by Faith under the Leadership of the Late Pastor Dorset L. Smith was reassuring, comforting, and validating. Despite me yet being that fat kid when I had the microphone in my hand, no one seemed to notice my weight. Instead, they valued my gift. So, I quickly gravitated toward the oratory arts such as radio, TV, skits, speeches, and the like. When I was at church, my sensations and feelings of being quickly offended were abated because I knew that people knew I was validated by something I did well.

Let me take a moment to say that reinforcement from a child's home church family is very important. As a senior Pastor, I often stress to the congregation the vital importance of rooting for our youth, whether it's a speech, a play, or even a sporting event. I feel that we should rally behind our youth to let them know that win, lose, or draw, we love you, and we support you.

I played football and ran track indoors and outdoors. I also played basketball and volleyball. Throughout high school, I was involved in sports; every season, I was doing something. We would play at the visiting suburban schools, and the stands would be filled on their side of the field. Mothers, fathers, sisters, brothers, neighbors, and friends. It seemed like the whole town came out to support the suburban schools we played against. Just imagine how great those kids must have felt knowing they had the support and the backing of the people who loved them and that they loved as well.

Many of our dads were absentees, and many of our moms were very hard-working, single parents who didn't have the time to attend our extracurricular activities. But wouldn't it have been grand if some of the deacons, pastors, and other male church leaders had shown up to cheer on the church kids? Wouldn't it have been uplifting for the kids who worked so hard to make the team and who laid their hearts on the line every time they got on the court, field, or stage? Applauding their toughness and resolve to compete certainly helps to build up a young person's self-esteem. That kind of support helps to point them in a positive direction for the rest of their lives. I know it did for me.

I must and always will appreciate two church leaders who showed up and supported every single game. Deacon George and Mrs. Archie Bruce not only supported their two sons, Michael, a wide receiver, and Duane, a running back, but they also supported the whole team. We called them our team's mother and father. They would stand and cheer every game, home and away. They live in Heaven now, but I still love and appreciate what they meant to our entire team.

That brings me back to the neighborhood I grew up in. There I was, yet "Fat Boy, Jeff". On top of that, I was getting bullied constantly. I mean, I was getting jumped by two or three guys at the same time, and often, I had my lunch money taken from me. I can still feel the sensation of my pockets being turned inside out. Being jumped and robbed on a constant basis is, to me, one of the most humiliating things that can happen to a young life. To me, I had the best mother in the world, a mother that validated me, taught me, reassured me, and nurtured me. Still, with all of my mom's great parenting skills, I yet fell into the category of "the sensitive."

However, along with public speaking, a few more things pointed me toward deliverance in my sensitivity areas. Being a fat kid had certain advantages when it came to sports. For one thing, a fat kid can be hard to tackle, especially when that weight is combined with anger. The older boys in the neighborhood discovered that I loved playing tackle football, so when I played and played well, it did a couple of things.

1. It gave me validation and approval from my older big brother types.
2. It quickly made me realize that the other kids were just as human as I was.
3. It soon made me discover that there were real advantages to being bigger. For example, I could run most of those little guys over with nothing but my vigor, vim, and vitality.
4. It made being called a fat boy less and less hurtful because I began to see that in life, no matter what your state was, there were certain advantages and disadvantages.

To this day, I yet encourage parents (and the children) to allow their children to play sports. I found that sports build both character and self-esteem in children.

Chapter 7

Going to War to Gain Peace

• • •

As oxymoronic as it seems, many times in this life we must engage in war in order to gain peace. Let's begin with the premise that peace is not a natural or innate condition of humanity. In other words, because of the sinful fall of mankind, because of Adam's sin, mankind in his natural or left alone state is anti-God. Our nature is predisposed to sin, to lying, to cussing, to fighting. That sin nature is also inclined to being led by feelings and emotions like hatred, fear, envy, and laziness. It is geared toward behaviors like being conniving and even toward hurtfulness or being offended.

Think about it: Was it not the spirit of offense that entered Adam and Eve and caused them to be overwhelmed by feeling slighted or shortchanged by God? Adam's sin caused a separation between him and God. This separation was violent and catastrophic. It caused mankind to lose eternal life. The only remedy for this separation was the violent shedding of the blood of Jesus. He was beaten, stripped, spat upon, cussed at, jeered at, stabbed, nailed to a cross, and finally murdered. Make no mistakes about it, this was very violent.

Jesus even said from the days of John the Baptist till now, *"The kingdom of heaven suffereth violence and the violent taketh by force* (Matthew 11:12). When Jesus regained the victory over sin for us, He had to fight in the spirit so that we might have victory in the flesh.

There are many things in this life that happen and for them to be fixed or remedied, they must be fought for, combatted, conquered, and subdued. When dealing with the spirit of offense, and we all will have to deal with it at some time in our life, we must do the following:

1) We must recognize that what we are dealing with is spiritual.
2) We must battle in the spirit to have victory over it.

How, Then, Must We Battle in the Spirit?

First, we must understand that we are in need of deliverance from the awful spirit of offense and sensitivity. When we truly get sick and tired of always being in one battle after another, when we decide that our peace is worth fighting for and we don't mind fighting for it, then we will seek to learn what it will take to walk in complete freedom in Christ.

For our understanding, we must know that warfare and prayer are different. Learning how to bind and loose things according to the word of God is paramount. The psalmist David prayed to God and said, *"Blessed be the Lord my strength, which teaches my hands to war and my fingers to fight,"* (Psalms 144:1). Prayer is submission, sweet communion, earnestly requesting something from God. Prayer is also spending time with God. You go to God naked and unashamed.

Warfare is violent! It is going into battle and violently seizing back what you know belongs to you. Warfare is putting the devil in a headlock and commanding him to unhand your goods. Warfare is both binding and loosing and knowing the difference between the two. Warfare is verbally speaking to a spirit and commanding that it leave, submit, and be cast out in Jesus' name!

The principle of binding and loosing is that you are a spirit-filled believer and a child of God. You have the lawful right to command your environment and to call into subjection those evil spirits that are trying to control your life. If my emotions are dictating my life and I find myself on an emotional roller-coaster day in and day out, it's high time that I get a grip and go to war!

Fight to Regain Your Peace!

The Bible says, "He that hath no rule over his own spirit is like a city that is broken down and without walls (Proverbs 25:28)." When we allow the spirit of sensitivity and offense to be in our spirit, we also allow fear and unbelief to abide in our spirit. This causes unbelievable double-mindedness and instability. Controlling our spirit is akin to self-control, temperance, love, and patience.

If we are sensitive to our negative environments, we are like the leaves on the trees. When and wherever the wind blows, we will go in that direction. Are you going to settle for that or are you ready to fight back? I tell you that now is the time to fight back. Go to war for you and yours!

Let me clarify that I realize the sports analogy I gave in Chapter 6 only really helped to deal with surface issues of my sensitives. That sufficed for my early immature life, but as I grew into a saved manhood, I had to come to grips with a spiritual need for deliverance through warfare.

Psalms 144:1-2 says, *"Blessed be the Lord my strength, which teaches my hand to war, and my fingers to fight. My goodness and my fortress; my high tower and my deliverer: my shield, and he in whom I trust; who subdued my people under me."*

This word simply indicates to us that we cannot be passive and gain victory simultaneously. We must war for peace. I want you to know that you have a peace worth fighting for. Please know that Jesus went to war for us to have victory in every aspect of our lives.

Hebrews 4:15 declares, *"For we have not a high priest which cannot be touched with the feelings of our infirmities; but was in all points tempted like as we are, yet without sin."*

This lets us know that if Jesus fought through, we can likewise fight through and come out victoriously.

Allow me to explain what "infirmities" mean in the above passage. Being *infirmed* is not the same as being sick; there is a distinct difference. To be sick is to be ill but to be infirmed is to lack mobility, to be lame. The old-fashioned out-of-date terminology is to be crippled. Not sick, just lacking the ability to reach your God-intended potential.

In order to be free, you must fight back and go to war, even against your habits, shortcomings, generational curses, and sensitivities.

Conclusion

I'm Through for Now, But I'm Not Finished!

• • •

Let's continue this journey toward wholeness and confidence in Jesus.

I cannot conclude this volume without being sure that I have offered you the opportunity to receive eternal life. Yes, you can live forever, beyond any and all quirks, hang-ups, phobias, or fears! While God is working those things out in your life, you can be assured that He, being Jesus, has secured a place in Eternity for you! If you are serious about allowing God to have Lordship and authority in and over your soul today, whether this is your first time accepting Him as your Lord and Savior or you are simply coming back to him after having walked away, pray along with me:

"Father God, in the name of Jesus, Lord, I'm a sinner and I repent of my sins. I turn from my sins and receive You into my life as my Lord and Savior today. I believe that Father God sent You to die for my sins, and You did die for my sins. But in three days, You rose from the dead and carried my sins away. Now because of the belief in my heart and the

confession of my mouth, today I am saved. Thank God, I'm saved, and I have eternal life."

Praise God!

And now, allow me to be the first person to welcome you to the family of Christ. It is so important that you quickly unite or reunite with a Bible-believing church.

Tell others about your new life in Jesus.

Beloved, be on the lookout for Volume 2 of *Sensitive Saints: Overcoming the Spirit of Offense*.

I love you all, and I want you to --

B~N~Couraged!

Author's Bio

•••

Bishop Jeffrey Lee Melvin was born in Newburgh, NY, on July 26, 1962. He is the eldest of seven children. His mother, the late Shirley Jean Jackson Wilmoth, raised him primarily. He attended Rochester public schools, where he was a standout athlete competing in football, basketball, indoor track, outdoor track, volleyball, and Karate.

He attended a renowned Historical Black University, Central State University in Wilberforce, Ohio. There, he majored in communications and minored in drama. He also made the Central State football team and competed on the karate team. Melvin asserts that he learned more about academics and himself in college than he did in thirteen years of public schooling combined.

While in his second semester at Central State, Melvin dedicated his life back to Jesus Christ as his Lord and Savior. Upon his first summer break in his home city of Rochester, NY, Melvin heard the voice of the Lord calling him into the preaching ministry. That fall, he met and later married the lovely and beautiful Deborah Denice Jones, the first-born daughter of Pastor and First Lady Arthur Willis Wyreen Jones.

Bishop Jeffrey Lee Melvin is the proud pastor of two wonderful churches in upstate NY: The Power House Kingdom Cathedral COGIC in Rochester, NY, and the Encouragement Centre Church of God in Christ in Buffalo, NY.

He is the founding Bishop of the Church of God in Christ Rwanda East Africa Jurisdiction (Mother Merry Cherry Supervisor of the Women's Department).

Presiding Bishop J. Drew Sheard appointed Bishop Melvin as the Chairman of the Jubilee Broadcast Network, the media arm of the International Church of God in Christ.

Sensitive Saints: Overcoming the Spirit of Offense is the second book published by Bishop Melvin.

His first book, *7 Essentials for Tapping into the Veins of God,* is available on Amazon and Barnes and Noble.

Made in the USA
Columbia, SC
16 January 2025

51828784R00033